ON THE POOR

ON THE POOR

STEVEN KING

CALL OF CROWS

First published in Great Britain in 2018
by Call of Crows
Lyddington
Rutland

Printed and bound by Hobbs the Printers Ltd
Cover and text design by University of Hertfordshire Press
Cover image: hand study engraving by Charles-Nicolas Cochin, 1751

© Steven King 2018
All rights are reserved and remain with the author.

Steven King is hereby identified as author of this work in accordance with Section 77 of the Copyright Designs and Patents Act 1988. No reproduction, copy or transmission of any part of this this publication may be made without written permission or in accordance with the Copyright Designs and Patents Act 1988, or under the terms of any licence permitting limited photocopying issued by the copyright Licensing Agency, 90 Tottenham Court Road, London W1T 4LP.

Any person undertaking of facilitating unauthorised copying may be liable to criminal prosecution and civil claims for damages.

ISBN 978-1-912523-00-9

For Georgia, Ashlyn, Elissa, Maddison, Jorge, Ben and Arlo

Contents

Introduction   1

Dreaming	7
Wasted Space	9
Looking Through Diamonds	11
Charlatans?	12
This	13
Will You Please Oblige Me?	14
Brickwell Court	16
The Poor Forgotten	17
A Past	18
Generation Rent	19
Descent	20
Rich Kids	21
They Came	22
Making Do	23
Bob	25
Immigrant 70596814	26
A Nan	27
NH Death	28
Paul J.	30
An Evil Union Begot	31
I	32
Known Unknowns (Oxford)	33
Fading Away	34
Escape Route	35
Fallen Idols	36
A Decision To Do	37
Reflecting	40

Taxing Space	41
On You And Me	42
Ummm	43
Walk In Turn	44
Accounting	45
My People / A Poor's Voice	46
Whatever	47
Idle Talk	48
A Lesson	49
To Be	50
Apologetic Garb	51
Going	52
Seeing At Last?	53
Coming To An End	54
Steven King	55
Post Scriptum	56

Introduction

For the so-called 'baby boomers' of the late twentieth-century, rising prosperity, decently funded welfare and health systems, rising house prices and clear opportunities for social mobility seemed to have eliminated forever the grinding poverty that had dogged past British societies. There were wrinkles of course. The 1970s and early 1980s saw ideologically driven governments drag the country to the brink of collapse. Yet by and large the liberal elites who dominate our political life and public discourse have been able to trace a happy picture of improvement. Not, though, for all. I was one of those people left behind by this progressive story, stuck on a bleak Northampton council estate and going to a school where for any year group reaching the age of eighteen, more people had been murdered, committed suicide or were in jail than had gone to University. It was not meant to be like this. Growing up for the early part of my life in Oxford was not exactly idyllic; the extraordinary juxtaposition of an elite University, tourists and ordinary city residents constantly emphasised how the other ten per cent lived. Yet I was surrounded by my people and could always find somewhere to hide. I would never have made a brickie like my father, but I might have moved into the car factory or perhaps farming. The break-up of my parents — from a boyhood memory, a dignified break-up even though there was cause for it not to be — and my mother's taking up with a deadbeat of the vilest hue took me unwillingly to the vast new Eastern District of Northampton. There my present journey — a determined effort to get out and stay out of that place – took its shape. My growing up was peopled by the odd, the scary, the weird and a raft of scum, but also by the many good people who tried to build, or rebuild, their lives in these ugly brown terraces. I will never know how many succeeded in getting out and getting on, but I think all too few. We were largely out of sight and certainly out of voice, and so the local and national politicos could happily ignore us and congratulate themselves on their building of the 'New Towns' that they themselves would never live in.

Against this backdrop, I used to think of myself as a success story and to believe that with the right character, support and good luck, anyone could make the same leap. Not now. Over time the liberal project epitomised by Blair, Brown, Cameron, Clegg, May and Corbyn has lost its shine. Politicians have been reminded of this fact at times of shock to the system. Brexit was not a vote against the European Union, but against the liberal elite from all parties who had overseen the crushing of local and regional economies, and the systematic suppression of wages through uncontrolled immigration. The Grenfell Tower disaster was, for an all-too-short time, front-page news because lots of poor people died, but also because of the juxtaposition of extraordinary wealth and tower-block poverty side-by-side. Some people it seemed – companies, politicians and wealthy council-tax-payers – had been having it large while ordinary people – voiceless people – struggled. Arguably, these sorts of events mask a more pernicious liberal contempt for the poor. Since the late-1980s politicians, quangos and the pressure groups that support them have overseen a fatal collapse in the infrastructure that used to drive social mobility. The chances of climbing out of poverty if you are born into it have folded, while the triggers for falling into sustained poverty have increased markedly. Personal debt has (with the active support of the Bank of England and all political parties) reached levels that signal impending destruction of household finances. The welfare system is crumbling, in significant part because politicians lack the courage to remove the subsidy to middle-class life that the NHS in particular offers and introduce a means-tested social insurance scheme. There is a housing crisis of epic proportions and house prices have reached such a level that any ameliorative action threatens economic crisis. An ageing population costs more to support than taxpayers are willing to bear. The British education system is failing on every front. Add this and more together and it is no surprise that social mobility on all conventional measures froze in the early 2000s and has gone into reverse in the 2010s. The 2008 financial crisis and its aftermath has not helped of course, but this is not the root of the problem. Rather, fine liberal words have translated to false action and conscious inaction.

Looking onwards, it seems plain to me that poverty in its widest sweep will worsen in the future. Students leaving University with the crippling debt imposed upon them by all three political parties will not take part in a renewal of the middling classes. They will inevitably be poorer than their parental generation, even if they manage the impossible and can afford their own houses. Employment levels are high, but wages grow slowly. In part this is because of low productivity, but also because international trade and migration in a global economy ensure we import wage deflation. The NHS and adult social-care services are not fit for purpose. They never can be, given that the financial model on which they are based presupposes them to be safety nets for the most sick and the most vulnerable, rather than the universal services that politicians have promised. And as people live longer, so they will live sicker. The 'problem' of the British and European welfare system will magnify inexorably. My poor tribe has not gone away. Rather, our numbers are being augmented inexorably every single year.

The feeble political system of the recent past has few answers: we have tried to extend the tax base through lots of sly and inept stealth taxes; politicos have named and shamed companies and public-sector bodies where workers and leaders have been feasting while social mobility reverses; Chancellors have closed tax loopholes and reduced allowances, cut entitlements and cynically manipulated the inflation uprating of all sorts of benefits, substituting RPI inflation factor with the much lower and more consistent CPI; the middling classes have connived with politicians in the mantra that those with the broadest shoulders will pay more towards the budget deficit, when in fact their bills have hardly moved. The rise of Jeremy Corbyn is a symbol of the failure of such politics. Yet his own solutions are equally inept, based largely on the fantasy that there are lots of rich people out there who can and will pay more tax to balance outlandish spending pledges. The liberal elites have conveniently forgotten that national debt in Britain is rising to impossibly high absolute levels because the system is broken. No amount of moving the tax-and-spend deckchairs is going, in the end, to help. The poor will get poorer and much more numerous because the liberal project has failed.

It does not have to be this way, but a new canvas is beyond the capabilities of those who (in the loosest sense) 'lead' our political systems and public life. This disease is not unique to us. In Europe and the Americas, poor people – ordinary people – are rejecting the liberal narrative and electing inconvenient leaders or parties, and seeking the break-up of states. The rejection of globalisation, free-trade and open(ish) borders is spreading rapidly. The British, as their history dictates, will be towards the end of the revolutionary queue. In this sense, we still have time for a national conversation. We still have time to acknowledge the need for the most fundamental of changes. Tick, tick, tick…

My poetry should be read against this backdrop. I am not politically partisan. All of the current parties are, in my view, utterly feeble even if there are a few individual politicians on all sides who 'get it'. I have watched my brothers and sisters in their own struggle to get out and get on from the council estates where we started. They have done so in a system which is consciously and deliberately loaded against them. An older generation has pulled up the drawbridge to protect its loot while a younger liberal elite has lined its pockets at the expense of the poor since the later 1990s. Our current crop of politicians is the most egregious example of this situation. So I have watched my siblings struggle, and now I watch my nephews and nieces, to whom this volume is dedicated. Will they be poorer and less socially mobile than me? Yes. Will they be poorer and less socially mobile than my brothers and sisters? Very likely. Will it be their fault? Will some utterly vacuous public writers stick a label equivalent to the 'snowflake generation' onto them? The answers will, respectively, be no and yes. Our generations have failed these children utterly and completely. In our very British way, we did not get angry enough to kick out a rancid political elite, or inventive enough to refigure their daft projects. In this sense, I hope that the stories – personal and observational – that wind through my poems will make you think about the future of your own nephews and nieces, children and grandchildren. And perhaps, if you are in your teens and twenties, you might get angry about your own future. The poor are all around you, to be sure. But you are going to be joining them; you just don't know it yet. Perhaps it is time, to borrow a phrase from one of my own poems, that you were out at elbows with the world.

STEVEN KING
JANUARY 2018

Dreaming

I dreamt such dreams
as would delude:

adopted I at birth
not meant for here.

Rich Uncle X, lost
but with a Will for me.

Winning the Friday pink
and doing big charity.

A stock market dude
with an eye for China.

Digging buried treasure
from a map of silver.

A mysterious safety deposit
box not yet broken open.

Keys to the heart of Lady Y
suddenly desirable I.

Lives not mine, but someone's;
a future not had but wanted.

A mind inscribed in fantasy
for the avoidance of a reality,

which rankles like a forged
note or a false word,

like a promise of one nation
or the word of a be-clad Lord.

My life's my own, but
why was it meant for me?

Wasted Space

The heaving clouds presaged rain
as the day met its crumbling conclusion.
Reason enough to walk on past
the old man hailing from his rickety bench,
hands as old as someone dead,
hard on a walking stick not his own.

'Did you have a good time at the Abbey?'
Words encrusted on a failing voice crept
quiveringly, begging a reluctant listener.
I reminded myself to be human and gather
them in, sitting at a still-to-decide distance.
'Brian,' says he, memoried eyes fixed on me.

And then a history, wittingly, splutteringly,
pleadingly given, layer on clinging layer.
Stories of old days, of memories dead and
people deader, trickling like dust from a mind
once firm and now ebbing like the Devon tides.
Yesterday became today, tomorrow and never.

'Brian,' he said, assuming I'd put his name away.
'Who are you and what do you do?'
My story exchanged, memories dredged, held,
and found wanting, a currency for the old,
freely given, for rehearsing to others who
remembered to be human and paused their lives.

Brian912@hotmail.com he proffered,
leaning over the still-to-decide gap.
You will contact me at some point?
A promise given; never kept.
A life told but not remembered.
Until now, but perhaps too late?

Looking Through Diamonds

Move closer. Closer.
Look through the diamond.
What do you see?
A great house with blinking windows,
white against manicured green and
the blue of a long-coveted pool.

And water, spinning in the air,
from a fountain deftly stolen.
Toys in piles, toys in trails,
abandoned, moving, broken;
bikes with bells, clothes never wanted;
all the things that credit can buy.

A boy, fine in his new waistcoat.
A girl, or perhaps more than a girl,
dressed in pure brilliant look-at-me white,
flicking water and running away
from a mother more manicured than the lawn
and a father playing out his begrudged role.

A family of four. Your own next door.
But not mine; or perhaps not yet.
Step back a little.
Now a little more.
What do you see?
A fence of diamonds, meant for the likes of me.

Charlatans?

I beg pardon for taking the liberty of writing,
but must know what you would have us do.
We have not the clothes to keep out biting
cold, nor food to fill the bellies of children who
must hide their have-not heads from others.
I humbly pray – will you weigh their
misfortunes in your heart? Think what a mother
must feel when power is gone and
punishing care sits leaden on a soul.
Nothing now left of dignity or respect; all
is brought to distress. So perhaps my liberty
might be excused, for how to lighten their
sufferings if not to impress upon your good selves
that we have done all we can and then some more.
But no more this way, a father and a mother
must make an abject call for needful charity
on their bleakest day. And will your Mailed heart
be moved to give or will you look on by,
congratulating yourself that you live and let live,
un-hearing the have-not children wondering why?

This

So we come to this;
the writing of an end.
My life seems rather
a flowing stream, at
once asparkle yet fleeting.
I was born an age too late
and a life too early.

Will You Please Oblige Me?

Music to buy for, untrammelled, loud.
A woman, old, cracked, bent, dull,
hands gnarled, a prime gone or never had.
Shoppers passing, trollies laden, minds not;
with eyes to see but not to observe.
Care less, care not, care for their moment.

A young man ticketing red reductions, then
a scrum, a push, a delve, a triumph;
honour served, a bargain not needed had.
A woman, old, cracked, bent, dull, watching,
waiting patiently in the tide of rushing loyalty cards.
A young man, uniformed up and ticket machine ready.

A piercing phrase: 'Will you please oblige me?'
Outstretched hand, shaking with the weight
of spuds now past a sell by date, past a prime.
Eyes which said 'please ticket me red',
and words of explanation: 'My pension just does
not carry these days, so please…'

A young man buttoned up, too young to comprehend,
hesitates, rules and rules marching through his head,
and feels sorry, good and guilty all at once.
A woman, old, cracked, bent, unnoticed.
Music to buy for but shame to die for;
a life shifting backwards, respectability ebbing.

A ticket of red; another gauntlet run.
But no faux triumph here, no boasting to be done.
A woman, old, cracked, bent, moving,
melting slowly into the aisles of possibility.
'God, look at her' (Mrs Blonde to a friend)
'Somebody shoot me if I ever get like that'.

Brickwell Court

Unbroken, unblinking, cheap in the morning sun, an endless terrace of Brown.
Cheap patter from the Council man: 'and warm-air central heating and double-glazing too, just finished, not what you are used to, I bet, in at the start of it'.
Misfit faces watch behind misfit curtains; a dog pisses in contempt. Brown.
And here we stand, keys in hand, not quite comprehending what we lost forever.
Look here now, past the cheapest words: a terrace to hold those broken dreams.

Bare floorboards in the codling cold of winter. The Council man adds warm air
to his list of ills, growing room by tatty room, red for urgent and Brown
for repair, eventually at least. My space here, his space there. Her space? Well, everywhere. Walking round becomes shrinking down for there are five of us to share. But share what? The money's gone, marching out with lies and cheating wives. Look here now past the tatty facade: a terrace to hold our broken lives.

And so our carpets come. Thin and grudging, fitted to boards that lift. Brown, like shit.
What chance here for me, or you, or them? No police, no Council, no school and no hope, just as it was designed to be. A terrace to mark our place and keep us at that 'not-me' arm's length, contained, constrained, cowed. A terrace of Brown to break our hope; a life sentence without trial and appeal.

Brickwell Court, the end of things.

The Poor Forgotten

I met today 1300 deaf ears,
listening candidly, earnestly
but hearing not a thing.
Their wearers? The crop of 2015
huffing and puffing deafly words.
A harvest of weeds not flowers.

I met today 1300 blind eyes,
watching, determined, honed
but seeing not a thing.
Blinking through, around, past,
careful not to make a difference.
A harvest of Elder when Oak was needed.

I met today 650 smooth tongues,
clacking, baiting, baying, soothing
but telling not a truth. Fragile
words from sharpened mouths
long trained in the skill of half lies.
A harvest of rhetoric, principle not required.

I met today 650 closed minds,
dreaming honeyed stories of heroic change
but understanding not a thing, hoping
now to glide serenely by those most
awkward of questions to the safest port.
A harvest of mediocrity. The poor abandoned.

A Past

Too old for this skin.

Too young for this life.

Too slight for lifting Mum.

Too alone for giving up.

Too tired for talking me.

Too tied for that chance.

Too much for young shoulders.

Too silent for real change.

Life cut down for a careless State.

Generation Rent

Faces, a sea of young faces,
the 'mature' long since defeated.
Faces: hopeful, interested, bored, resigned,
here by intent, dissent or just 'don't know'.
Customers, the aspirant future, buying
their degrees and hoping for the best.

Faces, their owners poorer now that
ladder-raising Oxbridge fools have
figured loans from grants. A breath-taking
act of false accounting to fashion a triple lock
for the unworthy old, cloaked in a sultry myth
of broad shoulders and accrued benefits.

Faces, distressed soon enough: 'graduate' jobs
masquerading in car hire, cleaning and charity,
the privilege of which paid at 9% for generation rent.
No chance of that deposit; debt aplenty for the
aspirant 20s; social mobility in reverse and meant to be;
futures handed to the old by shocking cowardice.

Faces, hopeful, interested, but misled, defeat looming.
No retirement here, nor prospect of buying one.
The old, husks inexorably hollowed by decay, sucking
greedily on the lifeblood of a generation left behind.
A sea of debt held in a net, waiting to close on the hapless young.
A gagging of politicians, defiling the memory of social mobility.

Descent

My fears, rough bestrewn on the tide of a black mood,
bob uneasily, waiting with a sticky embrace
to breach my intended veil, so tightly pulled,
and crash upon a fairy story, well-acted but still
gilded with memories of a history not so easily forgot.

Fear of falling, this, of slippery descent, of decline
to the terraced buckets of broken dreams and the
company of people, parodies of themselves, desperate,
despairing of lives at another's behest. Cold figures
creeping now from cold memories never shared.

A shadow, you see, of life stripped bare. An imitation,
lengthening into a future once thought my own,
yet somehow borrowed, on account, negotiable,
reversible, strapped firmly to a debt still out,
built on oily foundations that smooth the passage back.

A fear, you know, of that sharp still-life that I style
my own, melting, dripping, ebbing, soluble, and at
last fragile in the cold rain of self-doubt.
For those of us with riches must always know that
riches sometimes make themselves wings and fly away.

Fears, black now on a black tide, insistent, and creeping
silently over a life gathered in, celebrated once, but now
in the blink of a mind, undone. A tide laden with the
sediment of poverty, clings, saps confidence in a dark embrace.
Look down; look hard; see the wreckage; fear descent.

Rich Kids

His sheepish, shoe-brushing look
betrayed a secret worth explication.
'Explain' – a winkling word – 'why
you cannot be in my lectures at nine?'
His hesitant words crumbled in mid-air.
Camouflage gave way to concealment
and then admission. 'It's just,' said he,
'there is trouble getting out of bed.'
The early-worm inquisitor looked askance.
'No alarm clock here? Perhaps buy two, or
shall I lend you mine?' But no good such
words for they too crumbled in the great
gulf of understanding and sentiment unseen,
unspoken, unknown but somehow there as
something wrong, awkward, imprecise. 'It's
not that, you know, clocks, it's about getting
dressed.' The words simmered in the icy gap
between us, not more than two feet and yet
a lifetime and a history. 'But arms and legs
and eyes and hands all seem present and
correct,' even if rugby-like configured. And
then the punchline, opening like a sinkhole
or sink estate before disbelieving ears and
a heart sagging like a rotting log: 'We have
servants at home for that sort of thing.'
His sheepish shoe-brushing glance, showed good
grace at least to know there were no bridges.
Here at last, in a gilded political fantasy of a
bloated ex-poly, we came to the heart of it:
The poor had no place there.

They Came

They came for the whore,
crunching through the plated door,
applying handcuffs, lock and key,
as local husbands shrugged not me.

They came for the benefit cheat
in a clatter of early morning feet,
bundled quickly for prevention of fuss
as neighbours muttered 'not us'.

They came for the man of colour,
policemen masked in their mock valour,
thrown in the van for swift removal
as neighbours nodded their approval

They came for the beating bloke,
always high on meth and coke,
destined for the highest courts with
neighbours spinning do-nothing snorts.

They came to take her kids,
living no better than the pigs,
dragged bewildered, a social worker's prize,
neighbours looking on unsurprised.

They did not come for us,
the easy-picking Northampton fuzz.
But unease walked boldly nonetheless
at this select council-estate address.

Making Do

'Three jobs, you see,'
transvestite cleaner to the
Don. 'Three jobs just
to make ends meet.'

'It's expensive here and,
you know, for someone
like me nothing works,
I can't get on.'

'Trying though to climb,
you know, waking every
day thinking it will
come round, with help.'

'But no time for new
stories, nor old ones
come to that. I'll
meet someone, I think.'

'That's the key, see,
to be a couple, well
sort of, you understand,
working together as one.'

'There's the chance for
me because the State
won't give an eye
or a damn neither.'

'But it's so expensive
here and me not
well, not ill, but
just not somehow right.'

'Three jobs, you see,
so time is tight, must
get on, thanks for
listening to my story.'

A look back avoided,
then no more, not
today nor ever. Dead
for difference that night.

Bob

This form to fill, even though you're ill,
for those working-credit thingamijills.
Twenty-eight pages to shape your fate, all
freighted with the power of this feeble State.
Don't understand, can't read or write?
Time, my friend, to go to Citizens Advice.

But when it's wrong, the letters of the law
wing their poison way to your front door.
To hound and worry and drown a man,
because these faceless fools know they can.
Please attend an interview under caution,
so that we can continue our extortion.

Our scene is set in these Council chambers,
and you may foreshadow the lurking dangers.
A Suit offers no greeting but drips presumed guilt,
innocence swept asunder under a case lovingly built.
With a mind barely befitting the term, 'I think…,'
he starts in hapless fashion. Then falters, blinks.

A companion son to be ignored
until the title Professor is called,
and then an edgy panic ensues.
Browbeating guilt now un-presumed.
A case clearly argued, won and lost,
the public purse raided for a toss.

Immigrant 70596814

I am under the necessity to solicit
your aid at this time for I am in
great distress, having no bed to lie on,
but obliged to rest on the bare floor
and not the hope of any advance.
Gentlemen, I hope you will seriously
consider my case. I shall want little
of you, for I do not like coming
to crave assistance when I do not belong.
Do, Gentlemen, let humanity have a place
in your hearts. Consider if you were placed
in similar circumstances. Reason this way
and let things come home to brood
how unpleasant it would appear to you
but that our places be reversed. And no
person is certain but it may be his case
if he has power – well now sometimes
power ebbs and sinks out of speaking.
Alone am I in a land of wealth, splendour
and plenty. Friendless, voiceless, no history
or credit to draw upon. So, be pleased not to sit
with pockets full and your conscience empty.

A Nan

'You can,' she whispered in that
cracked and emphysemic voice,
'climb again.' The smallest tear
nested in the corner of an eye that would
close for a final time soon enough.

'It's not a matter of choice or chance
but one of obligation. You are the
only one who can, who can carry *us*.'
Then our little talk was done, brought
to a close by a smoker's cough and that
weighing and totemic debt to all of 'you'.

And now that she is gone, I have tried to
know and knew to try, to live those words
again and again: rise because you must,
for them as well as us.

NH Death

Tonight there was a drowning.
An old woman gravelling for life,
gulping in a sea of 'regulation',
laid to an airless rest by the book,
nurses too few, excuses too many.

Tonight there was a murder.
An old man, confused, sick, still
sent 'home' to unblock a bed,
flushed knowingly into a cobweb lie
of 'community support'. Murdered,
as surely as a shot to the heart.

Tonight there was a poisoning.
A woman in green old age, laced
with pills by a doctor out of time
and nurses out of care. Trust
broken but hidden in an 'Inquiry'.

Tonight there was a starving.
Tasteless ugly food dumped out
of reach, never to pass a mouth
arid with lack of care and in hands
incapable of grip or direction. Unaided,
left to hunger, but *sure* the food was there.

Tonight a woman passed by death's stare.
A doctor willing to go the extra mile
and a nurse not gassing but there.
By chance, good fortune smiled
on her postcode, and a life continued.

Welcome to your ghastly middle-class parody
where the poorest sink and the loudest rise,
where articulate lives are saved but
the poorest are lost. Behold not your NHS.
Welcome instead to the NH Death.

Paul J.

Lean in, lean in, I say,
and have an ear for this
secret story: I am gay.
No, I'm not taking the piss.

But I see it in your eyes,
a fear for me, your mate.
And I know. I can hear the cries
of this grumbling sink estate.

Woofter in our midst, a thing
of sport, a nancy to be shown
that being different here must bring
baiting words and fists being thrown.

This storm gathers for all to see
and so I look to you and ask:
old friend, will you stand with me?
I nodded and bent myself to the task.

An Evil Union Begot

Black and brown, red and green,
in all of these has evil been seen.
Blue and yellow? A sign of peace,
unless you happen to be hapless Greece.
Yet there in Brussels does contempt reside,
dressed in a flag and transnational pride.
Parasites with grasping hands a-plenty,
sanctioned locusts pillaging till 2020.
And so Europe's heart beats to evil,
the ordinary poor crushed like beetles.
For those who rise and tend to 'no',
must think again and again but never go.
Your elites have lost their will,
and left the poor to pay the growing bill.
Their lives wrapped in subsidy and corruption,
taking blind countries to the junction
of no return, when 'you' is lost and
'they' have power in their bloody hand.
So then you must gently grieve
for there will be no timely reprieve.
Now evil speaks with inflected tongue
to them or to us but no more to the one.
The Gods of Europe come to take their turn,
now watch with sadness your country burn.

I

I wished upon a star.
I wished upon the sea.
I wished upon a coin.
I wished upon a pillow.

I wished for cash.
I wished for love.
I wished for guidance.
I wished for hope.

My stellar wish stood unheard.
No one rescued my bottle.
My coin was taken in duress.
The pillow reeked with misery.

Hourly need stalked my waking.
Loneliness shrouded my sleeping.
No book of maps came to guide.
Hope a hopeless wish returned.

I wished for all but all was dust.
Faded flowers strewed my path.
I walked in fear and lost my way.
No low-hanging fruit came to grasp.

So my wishes became fantasies,
and chances slipped sprightly by.
I wished and wished but to no avail.
My life so poor was not to be released.

Known Unknowns (Oxford)

A need of shoeless magnitude
tumbled down that terraced street.
Grubby children grubbed for a chance,
yet chance made but a slothful way.
Distant, oh so distant, views of
whispering spires and mythic lives
filled our looking out. But this Oxford
was closed to us, closed to them.
Gown and gown but so little town
in this one-legged conversation.
And as these new freshers come to take
their comfortable and comforting measure,
what of those others, those Bartoned lives
cast to the doubtful care of keep-me-there
tradition? Nothing. Unless perhaps you –
wrapped in your resplendent privilege –
stop the performance of your evening
Parliament, gather up the dust of chance
and fashion it anew. For if not you,
who?

Fading Away

In this lull of tongues,
with others sleering round,
let me look at you once more
that I may tell a life.

Your fullest colour is struck out.
A thin and stingy air
holds fast, deep below deep, as
if you are hurried out of life.

Makeweight unhappiness seems hard
at hand. Those melancholy eyes
that once spoke of a philosopher
turn inward with truculent darkness.

Where stands the you of you and I,
and that tie of common funk?
The parquetry of words once we shared?
Our vapouring and fuming on the world?

Gone. Your shrunken frame
betrays the game of spice and
ice and all things nice. Your scrappy
edges hold misfortune tightly by.

So you stand, a poor morsel
of unimportance. The spaciousness
of times past stands now gathered in,
and the I of you and I must say goodbye.

Escape Route

You stand unready with your tongue to promise
that ounce of help or pound of acrid pity.
Your moment, vanishingly slight, flees
like that liquid morning blackbird, into the distance.
Where lies your debit? Not directly here for sure.
Rather, contempt stations himself and, bloated with
garbage, sends off into the thin and spongy air
your message: I am skilled in the art of looking
after myself. Please, please chug on.

Fallen Idols

£1000, so the label counted,
teasing, joking, mocking
my pocket clinging with absence.
And yet the picture hailed,
sighing as a wish of snipes.
Two heads of blue bursting through
a sea of green, rattling for breath,
pulling for a new life and place,
calling silently to one who knew
the turbulence of coming through, and
asking to be part of my mythical reinvention.
So the idea of buying ran, like a
slight of otters, until the clanking
grasp of poverty held my mind once more.
'What do you see?' A Canadian voice,
unbidden, drew 'myself' in involuntary
response: 'coming up for air; hoping
not to sink'. Grey eyes met grey eyes.
'But too much for me'. And then started
a pallid conversation, as of circling bears,
the meeting of which wrote out a deal
of instalments, of a bonded trust unexpected
by both. My life became by a degree less poor.
My class began to shift with that imperceptible
but oh so definite momentum, and as I walked
away my life was woven with a stronger weft.

A Decision To Do

'I just need that proof, see,
a statement of what's plain.
That I don't have any money.
I don't want to be a pain.'

'But it's just, well, like this:
I'm sick and not at work, see,
so they think I'm taking the piss;
them people won't let me be.'

'Yes, just a statement of the truth,
because my words have no credit.
So just some proper solid proof.
Yeah, I know the account's in debit.'

'I want to work, you know.
Oh no, of course, you can't.
I guess it's time for me to go.
I'm sorry for my little rant.'

Pushing past that restive queue,
daggered thoughts of the mad and fat
spilling out, she was gone and through,
the bank door closing with dulling 'thwack'.

'Fucking mental old bat,'
the Tweed to the brickie,
who grinned beneath his hat.
'She just needs a fucking quickie.'

Perhaps she heard or suspected,
as, on the other side of that open
window, she paused, sun reflected,
to sag and show someone broken.

And here she met my fleeting eyes
with that last-chance hopeless gaze,
loaded with such unvoiced cries;
an appeal for help with life's maze.

That smile, my smile of note,
broke there the frosty ice
and my heel turn was a vote
for a different kind of me: nice.

Said the professor to the bat
'I could not help my ears
So perhaps it's time we sat
And talked around your years?'

To stay or rush away?
That momentary peeling choice
circled in and out of play
until a deepest sadness took voice;

and she nodded loudly 'yes',
an assent to the telling of an
unfolding tale of spiralling distress
that left her so uncontrolling.

Our coffeed conversation ambled
across two lives and then was done
with the conclusion: 'Life's a shambles'.
And then she was, with a thanking nod, gone.

So next time you read of the re-invented her
in your must-see film reviews, remember this
chance meeting and our unballasting coffee-
shop tour. For life turns but on a word or glance.

Reflecting

I am out at elbows with the world.
Fugitive pieces of a life are yoked
together into something that smells
of success. And yet if I might, in a
confiding turn, tell you this: I do
not belong here. My life of masks
fits me out, but a personality of mark
hides self-doubt. Chance has been my
mother and mischance my companion
and guide. But now that all has come
to good I have no roots in any class.
Ghosts past die hard and a new self
lies part forged, never to complete. So
what will they say of me in a field of
stones defaced with supplications? That I
took the bootstraps and pulled to leave
behind a troubled start. But look closely at
these tumbling words, closer now, and
meet the eye of a stinking eel fix'd upon
you. This oh so sterling climb has
executed a dire and lonely sentence.

Taxing Space

A deficit to pay, with
rhetoric of broad shoulders,
the rich paying most of
contribution and of pain.

A deficit to hide, with
gilded words of the proceeds
of growth, shares of GDP,
and those un-subtle benefit caps.

A deficit to deny, with lies of
investment for growth, taxing
the absent rich, and those elusive
corporates finally hauled to account.

A deficit of what? Of trust,
of observation, of care, of
reality; and that slow, murmuring
realisation that you've been had.

A deficit of detail then, where
studied politico lies and arcane
deceptions crush the poor but
lets *their* valued lives alone.

On You and Me

You do not see me
clinging to the remains
of a shattered life.

You do not hear me
crying out for notice
beneath that muting pride.

You do not feel me
willing a snapped glance
or you-can-do-it nod.

You do not know me
though we meet unfailingly
every dankling day.

Twins you and I
in that morning bathroom mirror.
Yet destined for misunderstanding,

until the end of things.

Ummm

'Can you spare a moment?
Just a little help. You see,
it's beyond my thumbs,
these phone things and screens.'

And so I slid and pressed and spun
until his try-my-best fumbling stood undone.
My move to go was parried:
'You sound like my old motor.'

'That cough, y'see, not good
in one so young. It's a handle-
me-carefully day; am I right?
Come, sit, don't just pass me by.'

There I came to roost, as lazy as
a young crow, and he talked a
spell on the common confusions of
the world, with all the charity of a pig.

'Much wants more. And how can
it not be so? These rotten politicians,
feeble in their way, would argue with
an echo. The rich get richer and the
poor get poorer. All in each other's pockets,
you see, these gits; it can't be different
when such wood means such chips.'

Then our hour and two were put to bed.
But I listened to what this oldie said,
and now you should listen too: Your
pockets picked and you're all screwed.

Walk In Turn

Zip yourself back into that skin.
Pull back those mouldy curtains.
Sweep up the can't-remember wreckage
as this new day makes insistent cry.

I know you of times past, now pulled down
by the doleful art of nothing doing.
You've given up and given in, and all
that promise has turned to endless bling.

Can you rise once more? Can the words of
this watcher, focused with the intent of a
lunatic with a fly, take you back to that
time when nothing's lost and all is found?

Can we wind back our lives to understand
at last this place, this fate? Take my meaning
hand and come with me, that your skin might
once more be filled with an image of you.

Accounting

What point your account of me?

To bring the Press, shine a light,
and bathe us in the warmth of curiosity?

To voice the poor and confront the sight
of us as products of unwise alchemy?

To token need as worth the fight
and make a fellow figure for to see?

Or perhaps I grasp your politician's likeness right,
and your words mean to keep us in thrall to charity?

For our rightful share has taken flight
and your tribe has ridden us for free.

My People / A Poor's Voice

I converse with them as of old,
tightening the cord of a broken and
almost forgotten love, fashioning
together that past and some present.
To mind they come with their
wrinkling phrases so much treasured:
'Good dressing is oftener a sign of
self-respect than a weak mind'; 'You
should go for an evening dip in this
laughing ocean'; 'You look like a
horse with a Monday morning leg';
'There is no fame to be gathered
from the past'. These Baldon days
hold me in meaning, a man of exquisite
patchworks, unreadable even to himself.
I look again at this grave place: seditious
weeds riot and revel on dead men's bones.
My duty is undone. Yet still those mirthful
voices speak to the boy whose crying sowed
the wind to no effect. And I *am* here,
listening, walking once more this noisy
burial ground. Lest you doubt my story,
find us here under the name of Barrett.
My grave awaits and none too soon,
for as the tailor cuts our lives into sections,
somehap the pieces cannot always be
reassembled in that bearable order.

Whatever

'Whatever' drips with disdain.
A giving-up word, an argument
lost or never had.
'Yeah whatever'. Repeated for effect.
Macho shit for care-not, care-less, or
care not at all. 'Whatever', this
signature of no hope of change.

'Whatever' was never destined to jump,
and 'what if' never to be wondered at.
Yet what if?
What if you did not queue for the Next sale?
What if you did not play those fantasies?
What if there were no Maccy D or TGI?
What if you did not piss the £ on Friday late?

But, my Brother, what if stands beyond whatever,
and the one must give way to grasp 'what then'.
Perhaps to fly and soar, to have and hold, or to live
and laugh with people not like you. This picture
is not one for your bleak whatever world, and so
your gap life draws you now to tender embrace. Whatever
throws its disdainful cloak and becomes 'what never'.

Idle Talk

Do you see that talk of scroungers lolloping unsteadily by,
turning now to regard you with mouthing contempt?
No, of course, it has gone before you turn your head.
Yet you know it to be there. You feel it before the housing
officer opens her mouth. You smell its signature at the
interview room for DLA. You taste it in your paltry loaf
of working tax credits and that barely-there pension.
But what do you do?

The rubicund MP wafts his mournful parade of words
around his constituents. Fragile words of past success,
of sympathy, of action, of commitments to the barely managing.
The thinnest of words, soonest spoken and then haply gone.
He sits exposed, an emblem of his sort, of his people,
comfortable atop that majority that makes your life
and struggles nought but a whisper, a wrinkle or the slightest sigh.
But what do you do?

You moan of course or look for the 'other'. And you set the
world to rights every dawning day. But their boyling vanity –
these oh so liberal elites – care not for the righting. Your
world is full of wrongs, plankton for these grazers. So,
arise now.
The clock ticks past a just measure.
Arise now.
Take your story back.
Arise now.
Join me in the making of a confusion.
Arise now.
For if not they'll soon press 'delete'.

A Lesson

Open your ears so that I might share some
recondite lore with your self yet to be.
For what's bred in the bone comes out
in the flesh with the ease and use of wont.

The dog will look up to you.
The cat will look down on you.
The crow will eye you with disdain.
Only the pig will regard you as a fellow.

You laugh at this of course, with that
interior way of casual youth.
But you will learn soon enough
that you cannot plait the fog.

Those warming words of getting on
will be vanished soon enough,
and you'll a homeling not a comeling be
in this elderly world not yours.

So do not spend yourself on deaf vanity,
but rather do your nephewly duty and
listen in to this, my very last, as you leave
behind those weighty anchors of youth.

Your dogging friends will fly from you.
Your catting neighbours will turn.
The crowing State will soar away.
Only your piggy family will stay.

To Be

A place dosed with despair;
clinging hope lumbering to freefall,
and new life seeded for its close.

Young lives in pieces, roughly
stitched in chaotic canvas,
drawn tight yet stretched thin.

Sentinel voices unthinkingly crushed,
grind hope into new decay, and
maggoty peers show the easy way,

And so to war with friends next
door, keening misery cloaked in
the gingering rhetoric of gang families.

Now look some more at a settled score.
A gangman's knife cleaves a heart
and stops this last conversation.

Apologetic Garb

I told you this many times ago,
in stern conversation long misplaced.
But tho' you listened with that dutiful ear
owed to my grandfatherly countenance,
yet you did not hear nor reach out to
join these words, on rocky ends founded.

And now you come again, long missed,
clothed in that apologetic garb that I might
suspect myself and take back those icy words
given that you are a fiery beacon of beaten odds.
Yet, here, as I sit with my timed and timely
end creeping greedily across this contested floor,
I say to you again: 'You do not belong to them.'

For when, dotcom like, your presumed fortune
thins and turns to smoke, blown to all corners
by the grasping wind that keeps our sort in place,
your chattering friends in their fictive palaces,
floating on that churning pool of lies and debt,
will join you in your melancholy descent.

Be sure, my son, your fortunes are but fragile mounds
waiting to be kicked by the casual foot of fate.
When this misfortune should befall, and you
wish that you had heard the klaxon those years ago,
do not the misremember these, my words of last:
'Turn to the people truly of your class.'

Going

The habit of doing
affords a twisting path,
meandering between truth and
lies and make believe.
But then those chances,
those so unaccustomed chances,
slip all too easily
through their inexperienced hands
as if subject to
the subtle pull of
a dwindling moon. They
vanish by ones and twos
and threes, so a life
closes over, wrapped in
its blanketing leaves as
the wilting flower,
not to emerge again.
Now look.
That javelin of failed
hopes has lodged in
its fatal place, and
the taste of dust
stills that tongue which
promised much. The habit
of doing turns too
easily to this fate.

Seeing at Last?

Pull up the chair that you might condole with me.
What strikes us down we two? Why, a death.
No, no, not Peter, Sue or Andrew. My own.
I hear your 'I've been had' laugh, but take heed.
What you see before you is as a shell, hollowed
out, resonant, abandoned to roll with myriad sands.
I suffered, of course, but you did not feel it.
I cried but you did not comprehend the tears.
I drowned in that cup of expectations of which
we both so hopefully once partook. Now
this familiar voice talks to you in that disembodied
way that once you laughed to hear. So push back
your chair once more. Shake *you* free. Wrap up
the sky and the memories of this room into your
conventional parcel, and when in times to come you
ply your expectations again, pause and remember me.

Coming To An End

I have the look of a hospital man.
My part is played and exit planned.
Come, toll that parting bell at least,
that I might come to my timely release.
Or perhaps you'll fetch my breath,
and we'll reach a concord of death.
I have not done what I should.
You have not done what you could.
But we can at last be friends
and hold those memories again.
Now consign me to this night of lost souls,
as those pendant clouds tear and roll.
But remember me and this soul advice.
With a chance to rise do not, as I, think twice.

Steven King

Here lies Steven King
of Baldon and of Lyddington,
who died away to stink
at some date of your choosing
and under some helpful moon.

His likeness you have discarded,
but he stands before you now
in these unfurling black letters,
sturdy in plainest sight.

His share was had but scatters now,
to what effect you will never know.
Yet remember this man of swans,
lying unvoiced, shackled in
some decaying box beneath
your free-to-wander feet.

As you stand here now, wrapped
in the reflective silence that is his due,
give hope of memory for Steven King
of Baldon and Lyddington. Hear
once more that signal call:

Bollocks to this.

Post Scriptum

This ever starting story ends,
for now, as it was begun:
In crossed words, blind eyes, and
a certain unpliable confusion.
No more to say between us, lest
buried voices betray that plain-
sight secret: your suffering poor.